T0162723

A Gilgamesh Play
For Teen Readers

A Gilgamesh Play
For Teen Readers

A Tale of the First Myth & Legend of Ancient Mesopotamia for
Middle & High Schoolers

Jerry L. Parks

iUniverse, Inc.
New York   Bloomington

A Gilgamesh Play for Teen Readers
A Tale of the First Myth & Legend of Ancient Mesopotamia for Middle & High Schoolers

Copyright © 2007, 2009 by Jerry L. Parks

All rights reserved. No part of this book may be used or reproduced by any means, graphic, electronic, or mechanical, including photocopying, recording, taping or by any information storage retrieval system without the written permission of the publisher except in the case of brief quotations embodied in critical articles and reviews.

The views expressed in this work are solely those of the author and do not necessarily reflect the views of the publisher, and the publisher hereby disclaims any responsibility for them.

iUniverse books may be ordered through booksellers or by contacting:

iUniverse
1663 Liberty Drive
Bloomington, IN 47403
www.iuniverse.com
1-800-Authors (1-800-288-4677)

Because of the dynamic nature of the Internet, any Web addresses or links contained in this book may have changed since publication and may no longer be valid. The views expressed in this work are solely those of the author and do not necessarily reflect the views of the publisher, and the publisher hereby disclaims any responsibility for them.

ISBN: 978-1-4401-1030-6 (pbk)

Printed in the United States of America

iUniverse rev. date: 02/16/2009

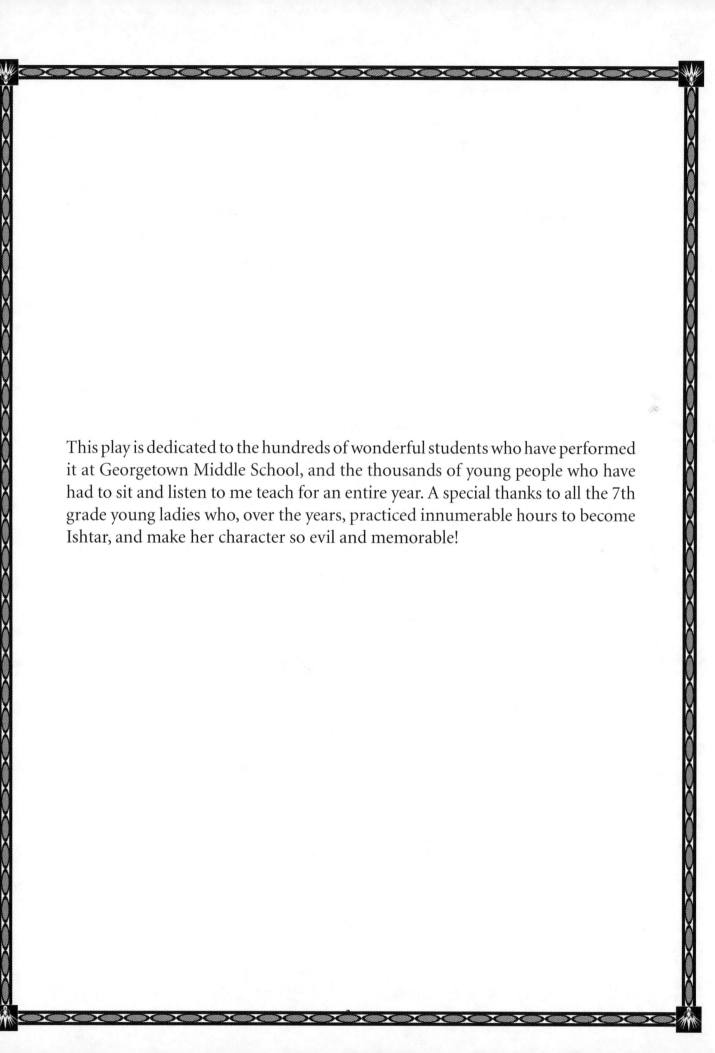

This play is dedicated to the hundreds of wonderful students who have performed it at Georgetown Middle School, and the thousands of young people who have had to sit and listen to me teach for an entire year. A special thanks to all the 7th grade young ladies who, over the years, practiced innumerable hours to become Ishtar, and make her character so evil and memorable!

Introduction and setting

The Sumerians lived in southern Mesopotamia (in what is now Iraq and Syria) from roughly 3500-2700 BC. They are considered the first great culture on earth. Living on the plains of the Tigris and Euphrates Rivers, these Sumerians were inventors, made war, loved gold, and gave us one of the oldest stories ever written—the story of the great King Gilgamesh. The area was known as the Fertile Crescent.

In addition to modern tyrants such as Saddam Hussein, the Mesopotamian area was also home to great historical figures such as Nebuchadnezzar and his famous Hanging Gardens of Babylon, the Akkadian king Sargon the Great, Hammurabi—the first great lawgiver—and the biblical patriarch Abraham, who grew up in the city of Ur.

In religion, Sumerians were polytheistic, and humankind was seen as subservient to the needs and whims of the deities. The following inscription says much about this relationship: *"Man is a shadow of a god, and a slave is the shadow of a man. But a king is the mirror of a god."*

As is denoted in this play, women were not afforded equal rights in Sumer. While slavery was not a major issue there, fathers sometimes sold daughters into slavery to repay debts. Sumerian laws could be very harsh, and government was by city-state and kingship. The king was called the *Lugal.* Finally, the concepts of sacrifice and covenant-making were held in high regard and with great seriousness in Sumer.

Purpose of this play

Because there are so few plays on the story of Gilgamesh written for teens, this play was created to fill the void. The play does not directly follow the original storyline of *The Epic of Gilgamesh*, and liberties have been taken in order to shorten and enliven the dialogue.

The play furnishes a great deal of insight into the ancient Mesopotamian culture, as well insight into the story of Gilgamesh. Probing questions on various themes for teenage discussion are furnished throughout the play, and those themes themselves are listed for the teacher's use. In addition, for quick-reference, a Sumer-cabulary is included in the back of this book. Words from that list can be found in bold print throughout the play.

The Story of Gilgamesh and Enkidu

The story is the legend of the great king Gilgamesh, and the eventual tragedy of his friendship with Enkidu—lord of the wild. It was written by a Sumerian, but was absorbed into later Babylonian, Akkadian, and other ancient cultures. Because of Gilgamesh's arrogance and pride, the gods created Enkidu—a warrior as powerful as the king—in order to teach the king humility. The warriors became friends and had many adventures together. But the evil goddess Ishtar punished Enkidu (and eventually Gilgamesh) with an untimely death sentence, and Gilgamesh undertook a long journey in search of Utnoa (Utnapishtim) the Faraway—survivor of the Great Flood. Utnoa alone had knowledge of the secret fruit of immortality, which lay under many waters. At the story's end, the fruit benefits neither the king nor his friend, but ironically, Gilgamesh—through this timeless story—has indeed become immortal.

Pre-teaching for the play

Before having students read the play, teachers should:

- ❑ Make students aware of the location of ancient Sumer.

- ❑ Discuss the inventions, laws, geography, customs, and theology of ancient Sumer.

- ❑ Relate the location of Sumer to news events taking place there today.

- ❑ Decide which themes will be emphasized in various lessons.

- ❑ Become familiar with the *Sumer-cabulary* in the back of this book.

- ❑ Familiarize students with the main characters in the story.

❏ Allow students to rehearse pronunciations of names and places.

❏ Assign roles appropriate to the reading level of students.

❏ Explain how students should emphasize certain terms and expressions.

❏ Research and resource other material to learn about the Sumerians.

Assessment during the play

At the end of various scenes, or 'Tablets', are probing and insightful questions which the teacher may choose to assign. At the play's conclusion are more reflective and summative assessment prompts.

Topics & themes in the story

There are numerous topics for discussion in the Gilgamesh story, as well as various themes, which may be discussed separately. Such include:

➢ Anger, and rash decision-making

➢ Astrology & Horoscopes

➢ Bravery and heroism

➢ Bribery

➢ Civilization of the wild: is this always a cultural improvement?

➢ Climate change in Mesopotamia

➢ Confrontation between adversaries

➢ Covenant-making and sacrifice

➢ Curses

➢ Deception and trickery

➢ Divine Right of Kingship

- ➤ Prophecy and foreshadowing

- ➤ Quest and journey

- ➤ Reconciliation of enemies

- ➤ Respect, and how it is earned

- ➤ Revolution against the powers of heaven, and the consequences

- ➤ Reward and punishment

- ➤ Sacrifice and humility

- ➤ Schools; ancient similarities & differences

- ➤ Selfishness and its results

- ➤ Sexism and bias

- ➤ Subservience of humankind to the gods

- ➤ Superheroes: their strengths and weaknesses

- ➤ Superstitious beliefs

- ➤ Tower of Babel/Ziggurat comparisons

- ➤ Trade and barter

- ➤ Wisdom and true accomplishment

- ➤ Women: roles, and male bias

- ➤ Work ethic

- ➤ Worship, and religious diversity

- ➤ Writing, and its development from pictographs

The 'Sumer-cabulary'

At the end of the play is a vocabulary of Sumerian terms and references which the teacher may want to become familiar with before beginning the play.

Disclaimers

A Gilgamesh Play for Teen Readers is fiction. Many of the characters, gods, and situations, however, are based on actual Sumerian records. While great care has been taken to create a play that accurately reflects the basic storyline of *The Epic of Gilgamesh* (the story of Gilgamesh and Enkidu), other characters, such as Utnoa (called Utnapishtim) and Harim (Shamhat) have had names amended for easier pronunciation. Many other characters are fictional, yet reflect Sumerian names. Also, due to often inappropriate content, and variation in the telling of the epic, some scenes from the original story have been omitted.

As a scripting note, this play is designed more for *reading* than for *performing*. As a result, teachers should feel free to incorporate any blocking sequences they might feel necessary to improve the action.

For further reference:

Gilgamesh: A New English Version by Stephen Mitchell
History Begins at Sumer by Samuel Noah Kramer
Picture-Show: The Fertile Crescent by the National Geographic Society
Sumer and the Sumerians by Harriet Crawford
Sumer: Cities of Eden by Time-Life Books
The City of Rainbows by Karen Polinger Foster
The Gilgamesh Trilogy by Ludmila Zeman

"A Gilgamesh Play for Teen Readers"
(A Tale of the First Myth & Legend of Ancient Mesopotamia)

Characters, the 'Tablets' (scenes in which characters appear), as well as the number of reading passages for each character):

Eridu: *Eleven-year-old Sumerian schoolboy* (**1, 2**) *{8 passages}*

Erech: *Twelve-year-old schoolboy who wants to be a priest* (**1, 2, 3, 6**) *{11 passages}*

Utnoa the Faraway: *Survivor of the Great Flood, builder of a great boat! He is the treasury of all knowledge that took place before the flood!* (**5**) *{12 passages}*

Master: *Teacher in the Sumerian Tablet house* (**1**) *{2 passages}*
Kainu: (the Stick man): *The school disciplinarian with the cane!* (**1, 6**) *{4 passages}*
Priest: *Offers sacrifices at the Ziggurat* (**2**) *{8 passages}*

Scribe: *Wise teacher of cuneiform* (**2**) *{6 passages}*
King Lugal of Ur: *in 2100 B.C.* (**2**) *{6 passages}*
Isharina: *Thirty-four-year-old midwife in Sumer* (**2**) *{9 passages}*

Nergal: *Thirteen-year-old Sumerian schoolboy* (**2**) *{5 passages}*
Hammur: *Thirteen-year-old Sumerian schoolboy* (**2**) *{5 passages}*

Gilgamesh: *Great hero & once King in Uruk (Two-thirds a god, and the greatest among men!)* (**3, 4, 5, 6**) *{45 passages}*

Enkidu: *Wild warrior & protector of the wild creatures* (**3, 4, 6**) *{16 passages}*

Serpent (and Third Stranger): *The sly snake who can walk upright and appear as a human!* (**6**) *{2 passages}*

Harim (Shamhat): *Beautiful singer/ servant princess to Gilgamesh* (**4**) *{8 passages}*
Ishtar: *Jealous goddess of love and fertility* (**4**) *{6 passages}*
Ea: *god of waters & wisdom; friend to man* (**4**) *{3 passages}*

Zin: god of fertility (**4**) *{3 passages}*
Ashura: *Daughter of Isharina (She's sixteen)* (**3, 6**) *{4 passages}*
Sarai: *Daughter of Isharina (She's fourteen)* (**3, 6**) *{3 passages}*

Inanna: *Daughter of Isharina (She's fifteen)* (**3, 6**) *{4 passages}*

(**Narrator:** *Reads introductions and* **bold** *'in-between' sections) {30 passages}*

TABLET 1: *The City of Ur, in Mesopotamia. A Sumerian schoolroom late in the day, over 4000 years ago!*

ERIDU: "Erech! Erech! Wake up before the Master sees you! Surely **Kainu the Stick man** will come this way!"

ERECH: (jumping up with surprise) "Oh, Eridu—I was dreaming of the day when I will stand high upon the **Ziggurat** as a holy priest, and offer **sacrifice to Zin!**"

ERIDU: "Well, that day is far off—you are only twelve. Did you finish your *cuneiform* **homework**? Hurry quickly—the Master is checking his tablet for our grades!"

MASTER: (loud and strong!) "According to my **clay tablet**, I may need to **visit the home** of one learner-boy this evening. I hope I will be welcomed as nicely *this* time as I was at *another* boy's home last week!"

ERECH: "Oh *no!* Hey Eridu— did you hear that Nergal and his father had the Master over for dinner last week?"

ERIDU: "Come on, Erech. Doesn't *everyone* know? Look at the new **gold ring** the Master wears, and his **new coat**! I heard Nergal and his father fed him **figs, dates,** barley grain, and fine vegetables! What do *we* eat here at the **Tablet house**? *Rolls!*"

KAINU THE STICK MAN: (suddenly appearing from nowhere, and scaring the boys with his loud voice!) *"Be silent, boy-learners! Aren't your **stone benches** uncomfortable enough as they are? Would you prefer to spend many hours standing, because you are unable to sit?"*

ERECH: (understanding what that meant!) "*Please* forgive us, sir. We have shown disrespect in this **Tablet house.**"

KAINU THE STICK MAN: (raising his cane with a stern look!) "You need to do more *learning* and less *talking*, boys. Perhaps then, the evil spirits that caused the **Great Flood** will not return and punish you *too!*"

MASTER: "Learner-boys, put away your **writing sticks**, and carefully put your tablets up to dry. Our day of **arithmetic** and study of the **gods** is finished. Your homework is to write each of the 240 **cuneiform** symbols **6** times each, and place them in rows of **60**. And do not come with the excuse of 'broken homework' tomorrow!"

KAINU THE STICK MAN: "And do not smear your **cuneiform** symbols on the clay! You must have perfect writing… (*laughing*). Someday what you write might be found by *future* people, and maybe you will become *famous!*"

ERIDU: "Oh no—homework…*again*! Look, Erech— the **water clock** has dripped all the way to half-empty! It's getting late. We must go home to practice our symbols!"

(The students place their tablets upon the 'shelf of dry air', and leave the Tablet house. It has been a long day of ten hours, and the warm Sumerian summer evening awaits them. So does their homework!)

TABLET 2: *A crowd has gathered beneath the Ziggurat for the evening sacrifice.*

PRIEST: (yelling loudly) "In the name of **Zin**—god of **fertility**, god who makes all things live and grow…."

SCRIBE: "…Excuse me holy **priest**. May I go with you up the **Ziggurat** to record the holy **sacrifice**?"

PRIEST: (acting insulted) "*What?* Don't you know, oh wise **scribe**, that our **law** allows only the *priest* to make the **sacrifice** at the **Ziggurat**? Maybe you should go to the **center of our town and read our laws** again!"

ISHARINA: (interrupting) "Be thankful, **scribe**—at least *you* can learn to write! You should thank the **gods** you were not born a *girl*!"

PRIEST: (becoming angry) "Woman! It was probably such complaining that caused the gods to punish us with the **Great Flood** which our fathers spoke of!"

SCRIBE: (agreeing) "The priest speaks great wisdom, woman! Perhaps you should be quiet."

ISHARINA: "You men make no sense. Wasn't **Ishtar**, goddess of **fertility**, a *woman*?"

SCRIBE: "She was. And what is your point?"

PRIEST: (trying not to laugh) "I think she wants us to think that women are important in our culture too!"

SCRIBE: (*not* finding this funny) "If the gods believed *that*, they would **allow girls to go to school!**"

PRIEST: "You know scribe, one would *think* Isharina might be thankful she *doesn't* go to school. At least she can't complain about homework!"

ISHARINA: (not enjoying being made fun of) "I may not get to go to school, but I do have *home* work. I work *hard* at home to keep our clay-brick house clean!"

KING LUGAL: (overhearing this debate) "By the way Isharina, where are your *daughters?* Are they working too, or standing around the town studying **star patterns to tell everyone's fortune**?"

ISHARINA: (firmly) "My daughters work the **canals** by the **Euphrates**, so that our crops may be **irrigated**. Without their work, our **crescent** would not be so *fertile!*"

KING LUGAL: (smugly) "This is *good*. Hard work is important. Oh, and by the way, what ever happened to your *brother*? Wasn't he a doctor?"

ISHARINA: "My brother was once a **surgeon**. Today, he practices the **law** codes."

SCRIBE: (being very sarcastic) "A practice that requires **less use of his** *hands*, to be sure…"

KING LUGAL: "Isharina, do you have any jobs besides keeping your house?"

ISHARINA: "Yes, I am a **midwife**. I help the women of the city of **Ur** to birth their children."

PRIEST: "What a *fine* job! The **gods** have truly blessed you, Isharina!"

ISHARINA: "If the gods blessed me, then why did they make it so that I can't go to school, too?"

KING LUGAL: "You ask too many questions, Isharina." (*The king leaves to sit upon his throne. The priest begins his climb up the many steps of the* **Ziggurat**.)

PRIEST: (sounding very tired) "I think I am too *old* to climb these many steps much longer! (Laughing) The **Ziggurat** seems to get higher each day!"

KING LUGAL: "Priest, is that supposed to be *funny?* Your job is *important!* How could we **keep the gods happy and fed** if you did not perform this service for us? Remember, only a priest can offer a **sacrifice** at the top of the **Ziggurat!**"

PRIEST: (wondering to himself) "…hmmm, If the **gods** *like* me so much, I wonder why they don't keep my legs from aching when I make the trips up and down the **Ziggurat**?"

ISHARINA: (walking away disappointed) "Women have *no* rights in **Ur**! My only life is to **serve my home and husband**, and tend to the women who are with child. I wonder what life will be like for women thousands of years from now?"

SCRIBE: "Hurry on, Isharina. Maybe you will do something *important* someday. We must get ready for Abraham to 'cut' his **covenant** with the king **to live on the land** for another year."

ISHARINA: (muttering to herself) "Huh! Do something important—*someday*? The wise young **scribe** must have forgotten that I helped *his* mother to birth *him* many years ago!"

KING LUGAL: (yelling) "Clean these streets! Your king walks here today! I shall prepare to **rent out my land** for another year! It is my **Divine Right as king!**"

(As Isharina heads home, Erech, Eridu, and two other school-boys—Nergal and Hammur—overhear this conversation, and make plans to watch the shepherd Abraham make his yearly covenant with the King Lugal. They hope to delay going home to practice their cuneiform as long as possible!)

HAMMUR: "Look! Abraham comes with his **lamb**!"

NERGAL: (sounding sick) "I cannot bear to watch this!"

ERIDU: (who has never seen the 'cutting of a **covenant**') "Watch *what*? I thought the **scribe** said Abraham was going to cut a **covenant** with the King? Will they not cut the agreement into **clay**?"

ERECH: (looking at each of the three boys, and then at Eridu) "Yes, Eridu, the **scribe** *will* cut the **covenant** agreement into the **clay tablet**. Whatever price Abraham and the King agree upon—that will...."

HAMMUR: (interrupting quickly!) "....*that* will be the price Abraham will pay the king. But *THEN*..."

NERGAL: (interrupting!) "...but *THEN*, there's **the blood**!"

HAMMUR: "The making of a **covenant** is a serious and holy thing, Eridu. An animal **must be sacrificed** to show what will happen to the man who **breaks a covenant**!"

ERIDU: "You mean—that **lamb** Abraham brings…. must *die*?"

ERECH: "The **lamb** must die."

ERIDU: "The innocent **lamb**—**sacrificed** to make a **covenant?** Gosh, what happened to just plain ol' promises and handshakes? I guess they don't mean much in **Ur** anymore."

NERGAL: "Come on, Eridu. Let us be going home. This is no place for us on a school night. Someday when we grow up to be men we will understand **covenant-making**."

ERIDU: "I'm not so sure I *want* to grow to be a man if I must kill an animal to make a *sacrifice*. They must take **covenant-making** VERY seriously!"

HAMMUR: "You bet they do, Eridu! And if you want to **live here on the king's land**, you had better take it seriously too. It is the Divine Right of Kings to rent the land! It is the way of men."

NERGAL: (noticing the growing crowds) "Friends, look—the traders set up tables to sell fine linen brought from Egypt. And look—they are also selling the clay **god-idols**, as they prepare for the evening **sacrifice**! Our street looks like a giant Sumerian flea market!"

HAMMUR: "I have always wondered why our people believe that the **gods** somehow *live inside* those **statues of stone and clay**. The people even pretend to feed them! Wouldn't a god be able to feed *himself*? And if we *make* the gods, doesn't that make *us* more powerful than our gods?"

NERGAL: "I have wondered about this too, Hammur. But we have *always* been taught this, and the people *continue* to buy them, so it must be true. **Gods** for this, **gods** for that…I just can't keep up with them all!"

Reflecting Back On Tablets 1 & 2

1. Why do you think Eridu wanted to be a priest?

2. List 5 things in the play you had already known about Sumer.

3. List 3 things in the play you had not already known about Sumer.

4. According to the play, what were 2 possible causes for the Great Flood?

5. Compare and contrast Sumerian students' homework to yours.

6. Compare and contrast Sumerian schools and students to yours.

7. What did the Sumerians think about their gods? How do you know this?

8. What was the priest's job in Sumer?

9. What did Sumerian men think about women in that day? How do you know?

10. What were Isharina's 2 best arguments to support her view of women's rights?

11. What were Isharina's daughters' jobs? How were their jobs similar to today?

12. What are at least 2 comments that show the Sumerian gods might not have been very 'real' to the people?

13. If Isharina could view our world, would she be pleased? Discuss 2 reasons why or why not based upon her comments.

14. How is Isharina similar to, or different from, women today?

15. Why is making a covenant called 'cutting a covenant'?

16. Why was a sacrifice made at the making of a covenant?

17. Based upon the play, how do you think people in that day viewed the whole covenant-making process? Explain.

18. Eridu and Hammur seem to have different views on the covenant-making event. Which do you most agree with? Explain why.

19. What did you learn about Sumerian trade?

20. What's wrong with Nergal's logic (reasoning) that since people keep buying the god-statues (idols), they must truly be real gods?

TABLET 3: *Nearing home, late in the evening.*

(The boys head in different directions for home. Erech lives near to the great Euphrates River—and farthest from the Tablet house. Alone he travels in growing darkness, knowing that his father and mother might be worried, and might also soon be inviting the Master (teacher) home for dinner! Crossing a canal near his home, Erech sees two large figures standing by the banks of the Euphrates, and a third standing in the shadows. Isharina's daughters continue to work late at the irrigation canal, and only later, notice the men.)

ERECH: "Excuse me sirs, why are you standing and looking toward the heavens? Are you looking for **wisdom from the stars?**"

(The men do not respond. The third stranger standing in the shadows answers *nothing*.)

ERECH: "Sirs, do you have names? Are you **scribes**? **Priests**? Workers at the **Tigris and Euphrates?**"

(One of the men turns to face Erech, and speaks in a deep voice. A voice sounding greater than a man's, but less than a god's.)

GILGAMESH: "I am called *Gilgamesh*—greatest of warriors, dreamer of dreams, and knower of secret things."

(The second man slowly turns. Erech notices that he is covered with hair, and looks part animal and part human. He is wild and tall.)

ENKIDU: "I am called *Enkidu*—protector of the wild creatures, king of the great forest of dark cedar trees!"

13

(The third stranger is mysteriously quiet. Standing in the shadows, he makes *no* sound.)

ERECH: (to the two men, and in a frightened voice) "Whe…whe…where do…you…co…co…come from?"

(The strangers look at each other, and then at Erech, and then stare up at the starry sky. There is no answer to Erech's question.)

ERECH: "Why did you come to **Sumer**? Are you here to **barter** goods? Are you here to watch the **covenant sacrifice**?"

GILGAMESH: "We came here to *die.*"

(Erech and Isharina's three daughters: Ashura, Sarai, and Inanna gather close by. They are frozen in shock by the appearance of the mighty men, and by the words Gilgamesh has spoken.)

SARAI: "You…you…you came here…to *die*?"

ASHURA: "*Die?* Are you going to *fight* each other?"

INANNA: (very upset) "Why do you speak such words? Why must men *hate* one another so much that they always fight and kill?"

ENKIDU: "Who told you we hated each other? We do not hate each other. We are friends."

INANNA: (Stuttering and confused!) "*Friends*? Did you say you were friends?"

GILGAMESH: "Friends."

ASHURA: (looking at the two mighty men in shock!) "I do not understand. *Friends* do not kill *friends*!"

ENKIDU: (looking up at the **stars**) "I did not *say* we were here to *kill*. I said we are here *to die!*"

SARAI: "Please, sirs, tell us of this strange story of which you speak. Why must you die?"

(The two mighty men, Erech, and the three girls, sit down beside the Euphrates River. The cool evening breeze blows down from Babylon, and chills them all. Gilgamesh and Enkidu begin their epic story. The third stranger in the shadows watches all—and says nothing.)

GILGAMESH: "Very well, here is my story. It is a famous story, and the oldest ever written. In the beginning, I was lord over a great city…

…one night I awoke from a bad dream…."

Reflecting Back On Tablet 3

1. Do people today still 'seek wisdom from the stars'? How? Explain your thoughts on all this.

2. Do you think the stars control/affect our future? Support your reasoning.

3. What is a 'work ethic'? What might be the work ethic of Isharina's daughters? How do you know?

4. According to the play, what was the climate like in Sumer?

5. Who might this 'third stranger' be? Why does he remain in the shadows? Support your reasoning.

6. Why did the children assume the two men hated each other, and were going to fight, when the men mentioned dying?

7. What is the children's concept of friendship? How do you know this?

8. Why do you think the three strangers came to the irrigation canals by the Euphrates? Do you think they wanted to tell their story to the children? Why? Why not?

TABLET 4: *The Epic of Gilgamesh*

(Gilgamesh tells his story, as all the children gather to listen.)

GILGAMESH: *"Harim! Harim!* Come and bring me my wine—I have had a *terrible* dream, and I do not understand its meaning!"

HARIM: (running to him) "What dream could *you* have—great king—that would make you so frightened?"

GILGAMESH: "In my dream I saw a great mountain. But this mountain was brought down, and, in being made smaller, became greater than before!"

HARIM: "Was there more to your dream, great king?"

GILGAMESH: "Yes, Harim. I dreamed the **gods** created a warrior as powerful as *me*! A wild man who speaks like an animal, and is come to *challenge* me to battle! I fear this may be Enkidu—the wild man you brought back here from the forest of dark cedar trees!"

HARIM: "But great king, he is *less* wild now, for I have cleaned and dressed him, and taught him the ways of *man*."

GILGAMESH: "Did you capture him with the help of men?"

HARIM: "I captured him with the ways of women. I captured him with my charm."

GILGAMESH: "Does he *speak* like a man now, or does he make the sounds of the wild creatures as he once did?"

HARIM: "He *speaks* like a man, but he only speaks of *fighting*."

GILGAMESH: "Fighting? Fighting what?"

HARIM: "Fighting *you*—oh king—greatest of warriors in all the land! King Gilgamesh, I believe the gods have created Enkidu in order to humble you from your great pride and terrible temper!"

GILGAMESH: (now showing his anger) "I have great pride because I am the greatest of *all* kings! I built the greatest and highest wall of any city, and the highest tower in the entire world—a **tower to reach the heavens**! None can defeat me! If it is the will of the gods—I shall battle this beast! Bring him! And let the earth *shake* and my power be known in all the land!"

HARIM: (seeming quite disappointed) "Yes, my lord. It shall be done as you request."

(On earth, the people of Gilgamesh's city cry out to the gods. Gilgamesh's great power and pride bring hardship to his kingdom. The Sumerian gods in the heavens are watching, and see Gilgamesh and his prideful temper!)

ZIN: "You see, **Ea**? Gilgamesh is *not* made humble by the sky god **Anu**'s decision to send the mighty Enkidu!"

EA: "True, **Zin**, but perhaps Gilgamesh will learn humility somewhere *else* along the journey of his life."

ZIN: "I don't think so, **Ea**. Gilgamesh does not realize that being only two-thirds a god, and one-third human, causes him to be *mortal!* Like all humans, he too must someday *die.*"

EA: "This, he does not yet recognize. It is hard for a king who thinks so much of himself to realize he is *not* immortal, as we are!"

ZIN: "Very true, **Ea**. I had hoped that **Anu**'s creation of Enkidu—strongest among the wild things—would cause Gilgamesh to lose some of his prideful temper!"

EA: "But he gets his strength from his mother, and his courage from the god of storm…"

ZIN: "…and his beauty from Shamash the sun God, but what about his foolish pride?"

EA: "His pride shall become his downfall! We gods will not allow mortals to think they are as mighty as us! Look! Even now Gilgamesh prepares to make battle with Enkidu!"

(Slowly, Harim leads the wild Enkidu into the presence of the great Gilgamesh, who has been watching from his great and high wall.)

HARIM: "Here he is, oh great king! I have brought him to you from the forest of dark cedar trees. I captured him with my charm. I have cleaned and dressed him and cut some of his hair so that he might look more human. I have made him as one of us—but no longer do the animals of the wild trust him. He has become like a stranger to them."

ENKIDU: (in a loud and powerful voice) "I have waited for this hour, Gilgamesh! The animals of the wild no longer trust me since I was brought to this place! No longer do I have a home in the wild! Now I must kill you for teaching me the ways of *man*! Only then can I return home to the wild and release the animals from the traps humans have set for them! Only after I kill you will they trust me once more!"

GILGAMESH: (also in a powerful voice) "Wild man, you do not look so wild to me. Did no one tell you that *I*, the great *Gilgamesh*, am lord of Heaven and Earth? A mere creature cannot defeat me, for I am *lord* over all things—even over your forest of dark cedar trees and its creatures. Yes, I am lord over even *you*!"

ENKIDU: "Only in your *mind*, Gilgamesh! No creature has *ever* defeated me in battle. You have no chance against my strength!"

GILGAMESH: "Prepare to meet the gods, Enkidu, for I shall kill you now!"

(Enkidu and Gilgamesh fight for hours, yes, even for days! The earth shakes, the lightning flashes, and the gods in the heavens watch as the two wrestle—until at last, both lie exhausted and weak on the ground.)

GILGAMESH: "Between us there is no champion, Enkidu. You are my equal. I cannot defeat you."

ENKIDU: "And I am not greater than you, oh mighty Gilgamesh! I have met my match. Let us end this struggle as *warriors!*"

GILGAMESH: (smiling and weary) "I have a better idea, Enkidu. Let us end this struggle *as friends*!"

ENKIDU: (with a surprised smile) "As *friends*? Then *friends* we shall be!"

GILGAMESH: "Enkidu, now I realize that *you* are the great enemy warrior I saw in my dreams! I fear the gods have sent you for a reason."

ENKIDU: "That may be, Gilgamesh. But I *also* had a dream."

GILGAMESH: "*You* had a dream, Enkidu? Could you tell me of this dream, my friend?"

ENKIDU: "Gilgamesh, I had a dream about a great enemy...but the enemy was not *you*."

GILGAMESH: (tending to his battle bruises) "I do not understand, my friend."

ENKIDU: "My great enemy is the **Humbawa**—demon monster of the forest of dark cedar trees. My dream told me that someday I must do battle with him and destroy his evil 'eye of death' which causes all the wild creatures to pass into **the land of shadows-- never to return!**"

GILGAMESH: "You mean the **Humbawa** brings *death*? I, the great Gilgamesh, have no fear of death!"

ENKIDU: "But I *do*; I am mortal. His mouth is *fire*, Gilgamesh, and he wears seven coats of armor!"

GILGAMESH: "Then let us *both* go to the forest of dark cedar trees and kill the **Humbawa!**" (Gilgamesh smiles) "I would much rather fight *beside* you than *against* you, Enkidu! The gods will protect us, and together, we will destroy this monster!"

(The next day, Gilgamesh and Enkidu visit the forest of dark cedar trees, and with the help of Shamash the sun god, and 'the eight winds', kill the mighty Humbawa. They cut off its head in victory! As they return home in celebration, Ishtar—goddess of love, fertility, and life—tries to *trick* Gilgamesh into loving her. She even tries to take credit for helping kill the Humbawa! Gilgamesh laughs, and he and Enkidu make fun of Ishtar for such selfishness.)

GILGAMESH: (screaming in anger) "Away with you, **Ishtar**! Everyone knows the trouble that comes to those who give in to your evil charms! Leave us! You mean *nothing* to us today!"

ISHTAR: (insulted) "Why do you refuse me, Gilgamesh? Don't you find me attractive? Or is even a *goddess* not enough to satisfy your great pride?"

GILGAMESH: (becoming more angry, and less patient!) "I said *be gone,* **Ishtar**! Everyone knows your tricks! Leave us alone! Today is our day of celebration for killing the **Humbawa**!"

ISHTAR: (smiling with an evil grin) "Tricks? What could you *possibly* mean, Gilgamesh?"

GILGAMESH: "All know how you were born from a great egg in the **Euphrates**, and went down to the underworld to visit your sister, allowing the crops on earth to die."

ISHTAR: "But Gilgamesh, don't forget—I went there to bring my son back from the dead! I have power over life and death—even *yours*—so be careful, prideful king!"

GILGAMESH (his patience at an end) "Be *gone,* **Ishtar**—you are *evil*—nothing but *evil!*"

ISHTAR: (insulted, and very angry) "How *dare* you speak to a goddess this way! It is true, Gilgamesh, as the gods have spoken, your *pride* shall be your *downfall!* I will send against you *and* your new friend the great Bull of Heaven! He will split the earth with his breath, and teach both of you *never* to insult a goddess!"

(The mighty Taurus, Bull of Heaven, is sent to punish the friends. Enkidu and Gilgamesh, still happy from their defeat of the great Humbawa, manage to defeat the bull, and throw its tail back in Ishtar's face!)

ISHTAR: (with great anger) "*Gilgamesh!* For killing the **Humbawa** and insulting a goddess—your friend Enkidu is sentenced to *death*! Listen carefully, you prideful king…before the month is over, Enkidu shall slowly waste away and join the dead **in the House of dust—the land of shadows**—*never* to return!"

GILGAMESH: (angry and hurt) "**Ishtar**, how could you be so cruel? I *command* you to remove this death curse from my friend!"

ISHTAR: "*Silence*, Gilgamesh, remember, you are only **two-thirds a god**, and in time, you *too* will join your friend in the **House of dust**—a place of great locked doors and eternal darkness—*never* to return!"

(Gilgamesh and Enkidu realize the words of a goddess must come true. They weep together. They try to think of any way to stop death from ending their friendship. Gilgamesh is grieved to the heart, and can hardly think of losing his friend Enkidu— the only warrior who can match his strength and bravery.)

GILGAMESH: "We have fought many monsters together my friend. In these battles I have learned the value of friendship."

ENKIDU: "Death is the worst monster of all, Gilgamesh. Someday, death will come for you too."

GILGAMESH: (**Jumping to his feet**) "Enkidu—I have a plan!"

ENKIDU: (sadly) "What plan can stop death once the gods have decided it?"

GILGAMESH: "In our legends, there is told of a great man who knows the secret to living forever. It is the man **Utnoa the Faraway**—survivor of The **Great Flood** of long ago! It is said that the **gods** have given *him* the secret to **immortality**—eternal life!"

ENKIDU: "You mean the great man who lives at **The Mouth of All Rivers**, and guards the rising and setting of the sun?"

GILGAMESH: "Yes Enkidu, that is **Utnoa.** He lives at the ends of the earth."

ENKIDU: "If that is so, Gilgamesh, then let me go with you, my friend, as you went with *me* to fight the **Humbawa**!"

GILGAMESH: "No, Enkidu. Because of **Ishtar**'s curse, you have only a few weeks of life left. Do not waste your strength. *Wait* for me here, my friend, and I shall return with the secret of eternal life. Death—the greatest of all monsters—must be defeated!"

Relecting Back On Tablet 4

1.   Why is this story considered to be an epic?

2.   Why do you think Gilgamesh is described as 'a knower of secret things'?

3.   If Gilgamesh was 'a knower of secret things', why was he not able to interpret his own dream?

4.   How do you think Gilgamesh became two-thirds a god?

5.   What was the Sumerian view of dreams? How do you know this?

6.   What do you predict Gilgamesh's dream of the 'high mountain brought down' might symbolize? Why?

7.   Why do you feel Gilgamesh asked Harim if she captured Enkidu 'with the help of men'?

8.   Why did the gods create Enkidu? Why did they feel they needed to do this?

9.   Was Gilgamesh wrong in his assessment of his greatness? Why? Why not?

10. Did Gilgamesh really feel he was immortal? Why? Why not?

11. Why was Gilgamesh's pride so insulting to the gods?

12. Enkidu came from 'the forest of dark cedar trees'. Describe your view of this place based upon the information.

13. Why did the animals no longer trust Enkidu?

14. If Enkidu returned to the forest of dark cedar trees, would they trust him again? Explain why or why not.

15. Was Harim wrong in bringing Enkidu from the forest of dark cedar trees? Why? Why not?

16. Why does Enkidu have such a strong dislike of humans? Why did he not show this toward Harim?

17. Did the 2 warriors enjoy/dislike their long fight? Explain your choice.

18. How do the 2 warriors now feel about each other? Why do they feel this way?

19. What did both warriors have in common in their dreams?

20. What do you think the Humbawa was? What did it look like? Why was its mouth 'fire'?

21. Use at least 3 references to describe how you think the Sumerians felt about the afterlife.

22. Describe and discuss Ishtar in 3-4 sentences.

23. Were Gilgamesh and Enkidu being unkind to Ishtar for no reason? Did they get what they deserved? Why? Why not?

24. Why do you think Utnoa the Faraway was given the secret to immortality?

25. Based upon the information given in the play, describe what Utnoa's home might have been like.

26. Why do you think Gilgamesh really didn't want Enkidu to go with him to see Utnoa the Faraway?

27. What did Gilgamesh mean in saying that death is ... "the greatest of all monsters"?

TABLET 5: *The Journey of Gilgamesh*

(Gilgamesh travels to the ends of the earth. He passes through the trees of precious stones, and around the black waters of death. He faces many terrible creatures, and even rescues a lion cub from death. At last, he arrives at the high mountain—home of the great and wise Utnoa. Utnoa is the *Keeper of Great Knowledge* and *Knower of Mystery*. He survived the Great Flood known as the *'overflowing of many waters'*.)

GILGAMESH: "Oh great and wise **Utnoa**. I am Gilgamesh, once a great king in **Sumer!**"

UTNOA: "I have heard of you, Gilgamesh. Wasn't it *you* who made life hard on your own people and recorded your mighty deeds upon the **Great Stone?**"

GILGAMESH: (embarrassed) "Yes, sir. I am that man."

UTNOA: "And wasn't it *you* who built the great tower that reached to the Heavens?"

GILGAMESH: "Yes **Utnoa**, I built the great tower even as you built a great boat to survive the flood. I wanted to protect my city and my people, just as *you* wanted to save people and beasts!"

UTNOA: "Do *not* think we are alike, Gilgamesh. I built the great boat at the command of the *gods*. You built the tower because you only wanted to satisfy your great pride."

GILGAMESH: "Sir?"

UTNOA: "My intention was to *save many*. Your intention was only to satisfy *yourself*. You may be a king, Gilgamesh, but you are only a *selfish king!*"

GILGAMESH: (in shame) "Yes, Utnoa, you are right. My pride was greater than my love for my people. But my pride has been brought down, sir, and I feel I am even greater now than before."

UTNOA: "And now, your love for your friend is greater than your pride. Isn't *this* why you have traveled so far to see me, Gilgamesh?"

GILGAMESH: (amazed at Utnoa's great knowledge) "How are you able to *know* what is in my mind and heart, sir?"

UTNOA: "I know *many* things, Gilgamesh. If you didn't already realize this, you wouldn't have journeyed here to see me, would you? What is it you want from me?"

GILGAMESH: "Please sir, could you give me the secret to eternal life so that my dying friend can become immortal and live forever?"

UTNOA: "Do not seek what you should not have, Gilgamesh. Death is a part of life. It is the will of the gods."

GIGAMESH: "But it was the will of the gods that *you* live forever, sir. Could you please share this secret with me?"

UTNOA: "Yes, I can give you the fruit of **immortality**. But understand one thing, Gilgamesh. This fruit must be eaten *completely,* and there is only *one* piece. Guard it carefully, and know this too—the fruit of *life* will also result in *death.*"

GILGAMESH: (confused) "Sir, how can the fruit of *life* result in *death?*"

UTNOA: "In the same way as the boat I built to survive the great flood, when the gods became angry with humankind. The boat provided *life* to those inside, yet resulted in *death* to those who refused to enter it. Only I, my family, and the beasts of the earth that we took, survived. I am the first father of all remaining mortals."

GILGAMESH: "Then…. you are my *ancestor?*"

UTNOA: "Yes, my son, and because I also saved the creatures of the wild by taking them on my boat those six days and seven nights, I have a *special* love for them, and they for me. So here is *one* piece of the fruit of **immortality**. It is for your friend Enkidu, who once ruled over these wild creatures."

GILGAMESH: "Oh, thank you, kind sir. Now I have learned not only the value of *friendship* from someone who was once my enemy, but the lesson of *true wisdom* from you. It is *you*—not *me*—who is greatest among the living."

UTNOA: "Your lessons are not yet finished, Gilgamesh. There is but one more lesson you must learn."

GILGAMESH: (confused) "Sir, what is the last lesson?"

UTNOA: "You must learn the lesson of *responsibility*. You must stay awake for six days and seven nights on your journey home. Stay alert and watch over all that is entrusted to you. *Responsibility* is the lesson of *kings*, Gilgamesh! Now the gods must test you to see if your *responsibility* is as great as your concern for your friend. Goodbye Gilgamesh. If you do not learn this lesson, you will bring sorrow to more than just yourself."

(Gilgamesh rushes with all speed back to the side of his friend Enkidu. He holds tightly to the fruit of immortality. After six days, nearly home and exhausted, the king stops for a cold drink from a mountain stream. He lays the fruit upon a rock, and falls asleep—just for a moment. Before Gilgamesh can awaken, a serpent crawling toward him steals and eats *completely* the one single piece of precious fruit!)

SERPENT: "Oh foolish mortal! Now it is *I* who shall live forever! Death will come to your friend! *Never* should you have taken Enkidu from the creatures of the wild, and stolen his purity! Now both *he* and *you* shall go down to the **House of dust** from which there is no return!"

TABLET 6: *Conclusion*

(The story being told by Gilgamesh to Erech and the girls is at an end. The evening has grown very late. Enkidu and Gilgamesh rise and prepare to walk toward the Euphrates. As they do, the third stranger in the shadows joins them. He has yet to speak a word, though he has heard everything.)

GILGAMESH: "So now my story is finished. As I told you, children, we did not come here to *fight*. We have come to *die*. Do not be sad for us. Be sad for yourselves. Though you are still young, in time, you *too* must die."

ASHURA: "*Now* I understand. You are here to die, but you shall die as *friends*—not enemies. Your friendship is as great as was your bravery."

GILGAMESH: "My pride was *greater* than my bravery. But now, our friendship is greater than either."

INANNA: "Wait, great king! We cannot *help* but be sad for you. Can the boys tell of your great deeds when they return to school?"

SARAI: "Oh yes! And can they write down the story of your travels, your great friendship, and the visit to the great **Utnoa**….?"

INANNA: (interrupting) "…*and* how you killed the mighty **Humbawa**?"

ASHURA: "Oh how *great* these stories of your adventures will be someday!"

GILGAMESH & ENKIDU: (sadly, as they turn to walk toward the River) "Yes, you may tell our story."

(**The third stranger in the shadows separates from Gilgamesh and Enkidu, and walks toward the dawn. Gilgamesh and Enkidu disappear into the Sumerian night. They walk as if their time is short, and they are looking for a place to rest—to rest *forever*. Suddenly, Erech *jumps* to his feet and yells with all his might to the third stranger!**)

ERECH: "Stranger—wait, please! Just one question before we see you no more!"

(**The third stranger in the shadows stops and stares at Erech with an evil smile…**)

ERECH: "Stranger in the shadows! You have spoken *nothing*—you have only listened and smiled. Must you *also* die with Gilgamesh his friend Enkidu?"

THIRD STRANGER: "Die? *Me?* No, foolish mortal, death comes *because* of me! I shall live forever! *I am the serpent who stole the fruit of* **immortality**!"

(**The serpent rushes toward Erech!**)

SERPENT: "….and now, I am coming for *you, Erech…!*

…for you, Erech…!

…for you, Erech…"

(Erech jumps awake from his sleep in the Sumerian classroom—his heart pounds within his chest as all eyes focus upon Kainu the Stick man approaching Erech, *with stick in hand!!*)

KAINU: "*...for you, Erech*, it seems a **home visit** by the Master is in order! I'm sure your father will prepare *wonderful* gifts and food! *Class dismissed!*"

THE END

Reflecting Back On Tablets 5 & 6

1. How do you think Utnoa the Faraway knows so much about Gilgamesh? Does he like him? How do you know?

2. What are 4-5 ways Gilgamesh and Utnoa are not alike at all?

3. How are Utnoa and his flood story similar/different from the story of Noah found in the Bible?

4. How do you think Gilgamesh feels in the presence of Utnoa? Is he right in feeling this way? How do you support your opinion?

5. Has Gilgamesh changed by the time he meets Utnoa? _Why_ do you think he did or didn't change? What are some ways you know this?

6. What did Gilgamesh mean when he said: "…my pride has been brought down…I feel I am even greater now than before"? Was this good? Why? How does this fulfill the prophecy of the 'great mountain'?

7. Utnoa seems to know many things. Did he really know why Gilgamesh came to see him? Why do you think this?

8. What did Utnoa mean when he said: 'Do not seek what you should not have, Gilgamesh. Death is a part of life. It is the will of the gods.'

9. Why did Utnoa really give Gilgamesh the fruit? What is your supportive reasoning?

10. Utnoa told Gilgamesh the fruit of life would result in death. How will this take place—what do you think will happen?

11. Why does Utnoa seem to care about Enkidu in a special way?

12. What did Utnoa mean by 'responsibility is the lesson of kings'?

13. Do you think Gilgamesh learned this lesson? What is your evidence?

14. Did Utnoa's prediction of death come true? Did it come true in the way you predicted?

15. What do you think Gilgamesh was really going to do with the fruit? Why do you think this?

16. Gilgamesh sought the fruit of eternal life. Even in losing it, however, he achieved 'immortality'. Can you explain how?

17. Why was the serpent so concerned that Gilgamesh had taken Enkidu out of the Forest of dark cedar trees?

18. What did Gilgamesh mean when he said: 'My pride was greater than my bravery. But now, our friendship is greater than either?'

19. Was Gilgamesh's initial feeling about Enkidu wrong? How do you know this? What do you think Gilgamesh (and you) could learn from this?

20. What do you think Enkidu said to Gilgamesh when his friend returned without the fruit of immortality?

21. Why do you think the serpent (the 'Third Stranger') was walking with Gilgamesh and Enkidu at the end of the story? Why would they allow him to? What is he up to?

22. Some things about the Sumerian schools were very much like school today. What are some similarities? What are some differences?

For discussion:

23. "It is Enkidu's fault that he must die prematurely. Gilgamesh did make a mistake by losing the fruit, but if Enkidu had stayed home, and never left the wild, he would have never had to worry about immortality!" (Explain why you agree or disagree.)

24. The making of a covenant was a serious agreement in Sumer. Often, it was as serious as life and death. For this reason, animals were sacrificed so that no one could forget how serious these promises were. Why do you agree or disagree with this method of guaranteeing that you will keep your word?

25. "Both Gilgamesh and Enkidu are to blame for death in the story. They should never have rebelled against the goddess Ishtar in the first place!" (Explain why you agree or disagree.)

26. "Gilgamesh should have left Enkidu in the forest of dark cedar trees, even though he would never have established his strong, lifelong friendship with Gilgamesh." (Explain why you agree or disagree.)

27. "Enkidu would have led a happier life if he had been allowed to remain in the forest of dark cedar trees." Do you agree or disagree? Why?

28. How you think the two hero-friends will 'go down to the underworld?' How will this story end?

"Our Sumer-cabulary"

Anu—god of the highest heaven. King of the gods.

Arithmetic—one of the subjects taught in the Sumerian schools. The Sumerians were the first to utilize schools, the plow, irrigation, laws, business transactions, astronomy, astrology, engineering, the wheel, the '6, 60, 360' basis for time-telling, writing, and surgery. They also invented the first 'envelope'!

Barter—to trade goods. The Sumerians did not have coins or money as we know it. They sometimes used tokens, and kept strict financial records in clay.

Canals—see *Irrigation*.

Clay tablet—Euphrates clay was used as a writing tablet, as well as for building. See *Writing sticks*.

Covenant cutting/covenant-making—a covenant sacrifice of a sheep or goat was made by cutting its throat when the covenant was made. This public ceremony showed the seriousness of making such oaths, and represented what could happen to the covenant-makers if they broke the covenant. See *Sacrifice*.

Cuneiform—cuneiform is 'wedge writing' because of the wedge shaped markings made by the impression of the stylus (writing reed) used. See *Writing sticks*

Divine Right/rent land—Mesopotamian kings were seen as having been given the honor to be king by 'divine right', or from the gods. As such, the land was theirs, and they rented it to their subjects. Kings acted much like judges.

Ea—Mesopotamian god of waters and wisdom. Ea was generally a friend to humankind.

Enkidu—wild creature of the forest, made from the clay of the earth. Enkidu loves and protects the less powerful wild creatures from the snares and traps of man. Enkidu has a strong dislike for humans.

Fertile Crescent—the area of Mesopotamia which was located by the Tigris and Euphrates Rivers. The most fertile area in the region, and crescent-shaped, when including parts of modern Syria, Lebanon, etc.

Figs, dates, rolls—foods of Mesopotamian schoolboys. Mother often packed these as a part of a boy's school lunch.

Fortune-telling—see *Wisdom*.

Gilgamesh—great, and sometimes cruel King of Uruk. He is two-thirds god. Gilgamesh is an unhappy king whose pride is never satisfied, and who does not understand 'friendship'.

Gods/keep happy—Mesopotamians were polytheistic. That is, they worshipped many gods. In ancient Mesopotamia, the job of humankind was to feed and keep the gods happy. Humanity was seen as in servitude to the gods. See *Idols*.

Gold ring/coat—Sumerian schoolboys often bribed their teachers by inviting them home to supper where they were wined and dined, and often given fine gifts in return for 'improving' the schoolboy's grade!

Great Flood—a great worldwide flood is a tradition in virtually every culture on earth, including Mesopotamia. See *Utnoa*.

Great Stone—known as a stele. See *law in the center of town.*

Harim (Shamhat)—the most beautiful woman in Uruk. She sings and plays her harp, and her skills and charm are mesmerizing to all who hear. Her beauty and charm lure the forest creature Enkidu. She teaches him the ways of men and brings him before Gilgamesh. Because of Harim, Enkidu leaves all he has ever known, forever.

Home visit—see *Bribery; Gold ring/coat*

House of dust—the Mesopotamian reference to death. To Mesopotamians, the afterlife was dark and gloomy. It had locked 'doors', was dreary, and appeared and rather hopeless. Souls there were as wandering ghosts. See *Land of shadows.*

Humbawa—the monster of the forest. The Humbawa (Humbaba) was a type of evil or demonic spirit opposed to what was good. His face was a coiled intestine in appearance, since the entrails—and gods/monsters—were often associated with predicting the future.

Idols/statues of stone and clay—these were the embodiment of the spirits of the gods. These were 'fed' by the priests. The food remained, of course, and it was said that the *spirit* of the gods ate the *spirit* of the food! See *Gods.*

Immortality—to live forever (eternal life). This was a great dream of many in the ancient world.

Inventions of Sumer—see *Arithmetic.*

Irrigation canals—these flowed from the Tigris and Euphrates Rivers. They enabled farmers to keep crops watered, and the crescent 'fertile'.

Ishtar—goddess of love and fertility. She was said to be born from a great egg in the Euphrates River, and rumored to have brought her son (in some stories—her husband) back from the dead. This resurrection and egg tradition gives us the name 'Easter'.

Kainu—see *Stick man*.

King—see *Divine right*.

Land of shadows and no return—what the Mesopotamians called death. See *House of dust*.

Law in the center of town—public laws—such as those of Hammurabi of Babylon—were carved into a large stone known as a *stele*. They were placed here, or at the temple, where all citizens could see them. Therefore, there could be no excuses for not knowing the law. See *Great Stone*.

Less use of his hands—see *Surgeon*.

Live here on king's land—see *Divine Right*.

Midwife—a sort of Mesopotamian nurse who helped other women to give birth.

Mouth of all rivers—the mythical home of the immortal Utnoa. Probably ancient Dilmun. See *Utnoa*.

Priest—as in all cultures, a priest was a holy man who helped others 'reach' the gods. He often sacrificed animals to appease the gods, and carried prayers from the people to the gods. Priests were especially revered in ancient Sumer.

Rolls—baked wheat or barley rolls were often the meal boys brought to school from home.

Sacrifice—the killing of an animal to show the seriousness with which a covenant was made. See *covenant.*

Scribe—a scribe was one of the most learned people in ancient Mesopotamia. Scribes learned and wrote the hundreds of cuneiform symbols in the Sumerian 'alphabet', and could be hired to read, since many citizens could neither read nor write.

Serpent—as in many cultures, the old serpent was a symbol of cleverness, evil, and/or the devil.

Serve my house and husband—women were afforded limited rights outside the home. They could not attend school.

Shelf of dry air—a location in the Sumerian school where the schoolboys put their clay tablets, containing their class writings, up to dry.

Six/sixty—the Sumerians based their units on 6, 60, 360, etc. From these, we have our seconds, minutes and hours arranged!

Stars/horoscopes/astrology—the Sumerians were among the first people on earth to believe the stars controlled the future of humankind. See *Fortune telling.*

Statues of stone and clay—see *Idols*.

Stick man—the teacher's assistant in the Sumerian classroom. He carried a whipping stick (cane) to be used as discipline. He was greatly feared.

Sumer/Sumerians—a name often used for the early people of Mesopotamia.

Surgeon—Mesopotamians practiced crude forms of surgery. However, if a surgeon lost a patient, he could lose his hands!

Tablet house/stone benches/no girls—this was the name for Sumerian schools *(the Udubba)*. Boys (and only boys) sat on hard stone benches from sunrise to sunset! School was year-round, but included a short vacation during hot summers.

Taurus—the mythological 'bull of heaven'. From Sumer we get this sign of the zodiac.

Tigris & Euphrates—the two great rivers of Mesopotamia—then, and now. The unanticipated flooding of these and other rivers caused much hardship to ancient peoples.

Tower to reach heaven—see *Ziggurat*. A symbol of Gilgamesh's great pride.

Ur—a wealthy city of ancient Mesopotamia. It was the home of the biblical Abraham, and was large and wealthy in his day.

Utnoa the Faraway—(Utnapishtim)—the survivor of the Great Flood. He—and the Flood—share many similarities with the story of the Flood of Noah. He is also *'the old man grows young'.*

Water clock—a clay time-telling instrument that dripped water at regular intervals. Possibly used along with sundials to tell the passing of time.

Wisdom from the stars, star patterns—the Sumerians were the originators of what we call horoscopes—fortune-telling based upon the signs of the zodiac. See *Stars*.

Writing sticks—reed styluses used to put impressions into soft clay. See *clay tablets*.

Ziggurat/tower—a tall worship tower in Mesopotamia. It was also a temple where many daily activities took place.

Zin—Mesopotamian god of fertility.

About the Author

Jerry Parks is a National Board Certified Teacher, and a member of the "*2008 USA-TODAY All American Teacher Team*." He has a Th.D from Trinity Theological Seminary, and an Ed.S degree in education from Eastern Kentucky University.

Dr. Parks has authored eight other books. "*With Joseph in the University of Adversity: The Mizraim Principles*" is based on principles from the life of Joseph the Hebrew in the Old Testament. "*Dragons, Grasshoppers & Frogs!*" is a commentary for teenagers on the Book of Revelation. "*God, Help Me Pray!*", and the "*God, Help Me Pray! Workbook & Prayer Journal*", are primers on prayer for new Christians.

His educational books include "*So, You Want to Become a National Board Certified Teacher?*", "*Mentoring the NBPTS Candidate: a Facilitator's Guide*", "*Help! My Child is Starting Middle School!*", and "*Teacher Under Construction: Things I Wish I'd Known!*", a handbook for new middle school teachers in their first year of teaching.

Dr. Parks teaches 7th grade ancient civilizations at Georgetown Middle School in Georgetown, KY, and is a regular speaker around the country. He is available for speaking engagements and professional development seminars. He can be contacted at kidztchr7@hotmail.com, or through his website: jerryparks.org.